1

GREATEST WARRIORS
GLADIATORS

ALEX STEWART

ARCTURUS

This edition first published in 2014 by Arcturus Publishing

Distributed by Black Rabbit Books
P.O. Box 3263
Mankato
Minnesota MN 56002

Edited and designed by: Discovery Books Ltd.

Library of Congress Cataloging-in-Publication Data

Stewart, Alex, 1950-
Gladiators / Alex Stewart.
    pages cm. -- (Greatest warriors)
 Includes index.
 Summary: "Provides students with exciting details, facts, and
 statistics about gladiators"--Provided by publisher.
 Audience: Grades 4-6.
 ISBN 978-1-78212-398-9 (library binding)
 1. Gladiators-Juvenile literature. I. Title.
 GV35 .S74 2014
 796.8
                        2013005691

Series concept: Joe Harris
Managing editor for Discovery Books: Laura Durman
Editor: Clare Collinson
Picture researcher: Clare Collinson
Designer: Ian Winton

The publisher would like to thank Britannia re-enactment group (www.durolitum.co.uk/) and Deeds of Arms (http://deeds-of-arms.
org.uk/default.aspx) for their assistance in the preparation of this book.

Picture credits:
Alamy: p. 15 (Nick Turner), p. 19 (BlueMoon Stock), pp. 20, 22, 26, 27, 28 (AF archive), p. 23 (The Art Archive), p. 24 (Photos 12);
Arènes de Nîmes—Culturespaces (Marc Fasol): p. 17; Britannia (www.durolitum.co.uk/): p. 4 (Dan and Matt Shadrake), p. 10r (Dan
Shadrake as a Thracian; photograph—petewebb.com), p. 12l (Stephen Knight as a retiarius; photograph—petewebb.com); Corbis:
p. 25 (Michael Nicholson); Deeds of Arms: pp. 10l, 14, 18; Getty Images: p. 16 (AFP); Shutterstock Images: pp. title, 7, 9, 13 (nito),
p. 5 (S.Borisov), p. 6 (Stanislaw Tokarski), p. 8 (Will Iredale), p. 11 (Only Fabrizio), p. 12r (Thorsten Rust), p. 21 (Iakov Kalinin),
Wikimedia Commons: p. 29 (Acquired by William T. Walters, 1883).
Cover images: Arènes de Nîmes—Culturespaces (Marc Fasol): top; Britannia (www.durolitum.co.uk/) (Dan Shadrake as a Thracian;
photograph—petewebb.com): bottom center; Shutterstock Images (Iakov Kalinin): background.

Printed in China

SL002498US
Supplier 03, Date 0513, Print Run 2355

CONTENTS

EXTREME ENTERTAINMENT

Gladiators were armed **professional** fighters in ancient Roman times. They entertained huge crowds of bloodthirsty spectators with their fighting skills. In deadly battles, they fought for their lives against other gladiators, condemned criminals, and wild animals. The more brutal the combat, the more the crowd cheered.

STABBING SWORD

The word *gladiator* comes from the **Latin** word *gladius*, which means "sword." As well as swords, gladiators used other vicious weapons such as spears and knives.

DEADLY ARENA

Gladiatorial fights usually took place in an **arena**, an area covered with sand at the center of an **amphitheater**.

COMBAT VENUES

The first gladiator fights took place in public squares known as forums. From around 50 BCE, as the violent displays grew in popularity, specially designed amphitheaters went up all over the Roman Empire.

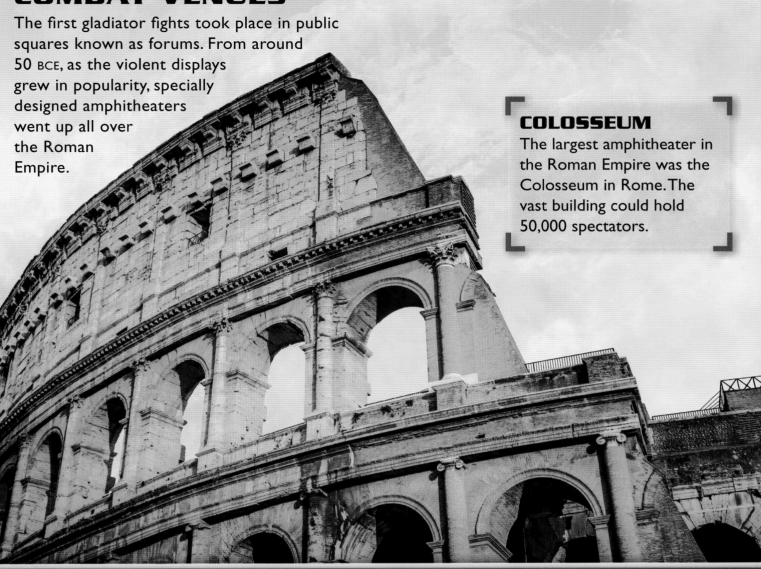

COLOSSEUM

The largest amphitheater in the Roman Empire was the Colosseum in Rome. The vast building could hold 50,000 spectators.

FIGHTING TALK

First gladiators

Rome got the idea for gladiator fights from the Etruscans and Campanians. These were Italian **tribes** living in regions near Rome. They held bloody "funeral games" (*munera*) to honor their dead. The first gladiator fight in Rome took place in the city's cattle market, the Forum Boarium, in 264 BCE. Decimus Junius Brutus staged the ruthless show in honor of his dead father. Three pairs of slaves were forced to fight, dressed and armed not as Romans—that would be dishonorable—but as **barbarians** from Thrace. The three losers died.

DOOMED TO DIE

Thousands of gladiators fought and died in arenas throughout the Roman Empire. The majority were slaves, criminals, or prisoners of war, who were forced into this fearful occupation. Most gladiators received some training, but few survived more than ten fights.

A DEADLY CHOICE FOR SOME

Some gladiators were volunteers who entered the violent profession out of choice. They were usually ex-soldiers or very poor people. They chose to give up their freedom in return for regular meals and the chance of fame, glory, and prize money in the arena.

DESTINED FOR THE ARENA

As Rome's empire grew, many thousands of prisoners of war were taken. The captives were often forced to fight as gladiators for the Romans' entertainment.

BLOODY BUSINESS

Gladiators could be bought and sold by wealthy Romans, like houses or slaves. A trained and experienced fighter was very expensive—costing perhaps 1,000 *denarii,* which was more than three years' wages for an ordinary Roman. And very occasionally a good (and lucky) gladiator made a fortune. **Emperor** Nero (ruled 54–68 CE) rewarded Spiculus, his favorite gladiator, with a fine house and rich estates.

DEATH ON THE SAND

A gladiator's training included preparation for an honorable death. Gladiators were not expected to ask for mercy or cry out.

COMBAT STATS

A risky profession

- **Risk of death:** Gladiatorial fights did not always end in death. When entering the arena, gladiators faced about a 1 in 4 chance of being killed.

- **Worst chance of survival:** The *andabata* was a gladiator who fought blind. His helmet had no eye-holes and covered his head completely. He was about 99 percent sure to die.

- **Number of fights:** Very few gladiators had long careers. Flamma, one of the best, had 34 fights, 21 wins, 9 draws, and 4 losses.

- **Average age:** Most gladiators died between the ages of 18 and 25.

- **Longest lived:** One retired gladiator survived to the age of 90.

SAMNITE—THE STABBER

Gladiators were divided into different types, depending on their armor, weapons, and fighting styles. Some of the earliest gladiators were known as **Samnites**. They were named after the tough mountain people of Samnium, who were at war with Rome in the fourth century BCE.

SAMNITE
Early Roman gladiators equipped themselves like Samnite warriors.

STABBING SWORD
A Samnite's main weapon was a straight stabbing sword (*gladius*) about 27 inches (70 cm) long.

LEG ARMOR
Metal leg armor known as a **greave** protected a Samnite's lower left leg.

DEFENSIVE SHIELD
A Samnite carried a large rectangular shield, called a *scutum*, to defend himself.

THROAT-DIVIDERS

Advancing behind his large shield, a Samnite tried to close with his opponent and then strike with his stabbing sword. The best target area was the face or neck—a good hit there ended the fight instantly. That's how the Samnite's sword got its grim nickname, the "throat-divider."

CRESTED HELMET

Samnites wore crested metal helmets. These protected their heads and made them look taller.

ARM PROTECTION

A Samnite protected his sword arm with a guard called a *manica*. The *manica* was a common piece of armor used by many gladiators.

FIGHTING TALK

A gladiator's fate

A fighter could surrender by raising a finger to the referee. His fate was then decided by the umpire or the crowd. Contrary to popular belief, if the crowd gave a gladiator the thumbs down, he was allowed to live. Thumbs up meant sword raised—death!

THRACIAN—THE SLICER

The people of Thrace were famous in the ancient world for being wild and daring fighters. Some of their soldiers had fought with Alexander the Great (356–323 BCE), the amazing Macedonian general whose army was never defeated in battle. The Romans loved having gladiators named after such successful warriors.

CURVED SWORD
Thracians were lightly armed. They wielded curved swords with blades about 13 inches (34 cm) long. The swords were short, but they were good for slicing opponents.

THRACIAN SHIELD
A Thracian carried a small square or round shield called a *parma*.

THRACIAN HELMET
Most impressive was a Thracian's helmet. The helmet had a wide brim and a visor to cover the face. It was decorated at the top with a mythical bird called a griffin.

GREAVES
A Thracian's leg armor covered all of his legs, up to the thigh.

IMPERIAL FAVORITES

The Thracians were the favorite gladiators of Emperors Caligula (ruled 37–41 CE) and Trajan (ruled 98–117 CE). It is said that when Caligula became emperor, he rode across a specially built bridge to his throne—dressed as a Thracian gladiator!

EMPEROR TRAJAN

To celebrate his victory over the Dacians, Emperor Trajan held a festival that included wild animal fights and gladiatorial contests. It is thought that around 5 million spectators came to see the violent displays.

COMBAT STATS

Emperor's celebrations

Following the defeat of the Dacians in the Danube region, Emperor Trajan celebrated back in Italy with 123 days of brutal partying (107 CE).

- **Gladiator fights:** 10,000 gladiators took part in gladiatorial contests as part of the celebrations.

- **Animal deaths:** 11,000 dangerous wild animals, such as lions and bears, were killed during the festival.

RETIARIUS—THE NET WARRIOR

The *retiarius*, or net fighter, was one of the lowliest of all gladiators. Equipped like a fisherman, he wore hardly any armor and entered the arena with just a net and a three-pronged **trident**.

NET
The *retiarius* relied on a net to entangle his opponent before jabbing him with his trident.

ARM AND SHOULDER GUARD
A *retiarius* wore no helmet, but one arm and shoulder was protected by armor.

THREE-PRONGED TRIDENT
A *retiarius* carried a long, three-pronged spear or trident. He used it to keep his opponent at a distance while trying to trap him in the net.

LIGHT FEET, QUICK ARM

Nimbleness was the key to success as a *retiarius*. Without a shield or helmet, he had to be quick on his feet to stay out of trouble. Retiarii usually fought against heavily armed gladiators, such as **secutores** or **murmillos**.

SECUTOR

Secutores, or "chasers," were specially trained to fight against retiarii. They wore helmets as well as arm and leg protection, and they carried a shield and a stabbing sword.

FIGHTING TALK

The fish-man

The *retiarius'* deadliest foe was the *murmillo*, or fish-man. The name came from the fish-style crest on the *murmillo's* helmet. This odd-looking gladiator had an arm guard, leg and feet guards, and a large rectangular shield. His weapon was a stabbing sword. *Murmillo* vs *retiarius* was one of the crowds' favorite fights, with the fish-man often coming out on top.

FIGHTING WOMEN

By the first century CE, gladiatorial contests had become lavish, weird, and horrible. They featured wild animals, dwarves, children, and women. Throwing females into the arena was seen as something special.

NOVELTY ACTS

In Roman eyes, fights between females made an unusual change from contests between male gladiators. Women were made to battle with wild animals or put on armor and hack at each other like male gladiators.

TWO-AGAINST-ONE
Women gladiators usually fought each other, not men. Sometimes they had to fight in two-against-one contests like this one.

WOMEN WARRIORS

Like male fighters, most female gladiators were slaves or prisoners of war. Scholars believe that they were trained to fight, but not at the all-male gladiator schools. They usually fought with swords and shields, and they wore arm protectors and greaves on the lower leg. They were rarely given the protection of a helmet.

BATTLE REPORT

Imperial horrors

The cruelest shows seem to have been organized by the emperors themselves. In 66 CE, Nero organized a massive battle between two groups of men, women, and children. Twenty-three years later, in the time of Emperor Domitian, a battle was arranged between an army of women and an army of dwarves. We do not know who won.

HORSEMEN

Gladiatorial contests mirrored combat on the battlefield. Just as armies had **cavalries**, there were mounted gladiators who fought on horseback. These horsemen, or *equites*, were the cream of the gladiators.

A FAIR FIGHT
To make for an even fight, *equites* only fought each other. The battles began on horseback but usually ended on foot.

SHIELD
Equites carried shields 18 inches (46 cm) in diameter.

BATTLE HORSE
In Roman times, a good horse cost as much as a new family car costs today. They were ridden without **stirrups**, which had not been invented.

ENTER THE BRITS

After conquering Gaul (France), in 55 and 54 BCE, Julius Caesar came to Britain. Here, his soldiers found a new weapon, the war chariot. Before long, gladiators (known as *essedarii*) were fighting each other from chariots back in Rome. Because horses and chariots were costly, these thrilling gladiatorial contests were the most expensive of all.

FIGHTING TALK

Deadly chariots

There are reports of some of Rome's enemies using "scythed chariots"—chariots with knives sticking out of the axles on either side. We do not know for sure whether scythed chariots were used in the gladiatorial arena—but if so, they would certainly have made the shows more gory!

FIGHT SCHOOL

Gladiators were professional fighters who were expected to put on a good show. To guarantee this, from 105 BCE, they trained in special gladiator boarding schools. Here, a gladiator learned to fight with skill—and to die bravely.

WEAPONS TRAINING
Gladiators were given training in different fighting styles and techniques. Students practiced with wooden or blunted weapons.

TOUGH TRAINING

At school, most gladiators lived and slept under guard so they could not escape. They were fed a special high-energy vegetarian diet of cereals and dried fruit, and they were given top-level medical attention, including a regular massage. Each group of gladiators (*familia*) was trained by a manager (*lanista*) who could hire them out for a good price.

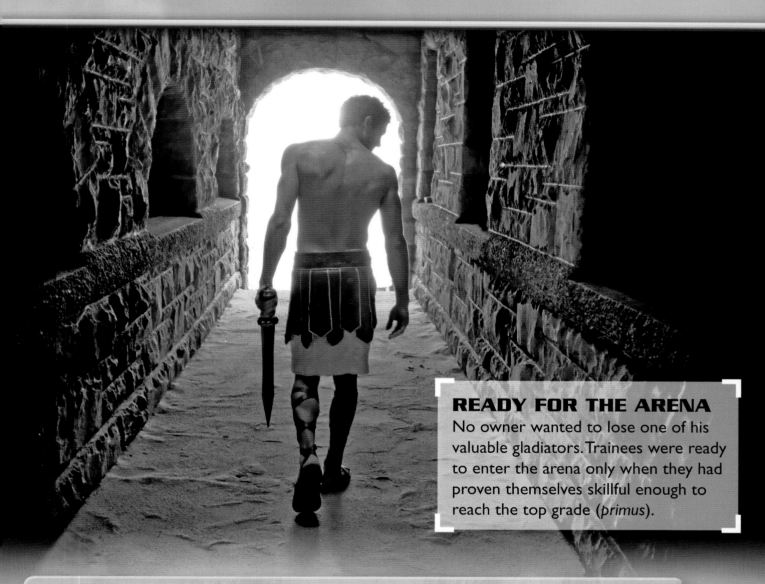

READY FOR THE ARENA
No owner wanted to lose one of his valuable gladiators. Trainees were ready to enter the arena only when they had proven themselves skillful enough to reach the top grade (*primus*).

FIGHTING TALK

A gladiator's oath
On becoming a gladiator, a recruit swore this oath: "I promise to endure to be burned, to be bound, to be beaten, and to be killed by the sword."

AMPHITHEATERS OF BLOOD

The earliest Roman amphitheater was built of wood in about 110 BCE. Larger stone amphitheaters followed, and eventually, there were amphitheaters in some 230 important towns and cities all over the Roman Empire.

BLOOD AND SAND

Amphitheaters were usually oval in shape. They had tiered seating so every spectator had a good view. At the center was the arena, a word that comes from the Latin *harena*, meaning "fine sand." The sand on the floor of amphitheaters helped to soak up the blood. On games days, pine cones were burned in special holders around the arena. The strong, sweet smell hid the stench of blood and gore.

ANCIENT SITE OF SLAUGHTER

The Colosseum in Rome, shown below, is now partly in ruins, but it remains an impressive symbol of Roman imperial power. For hundreds of years, this immense building served as the venue for Rome's spectacular gladiatorial contests, and it was here that many thousands of gladiators and animals met their deaths.

ANCIENT ARENA

The original flooring of the Colosseum, which has now collapsed, was laid over the stone and brick passages running underneath it.

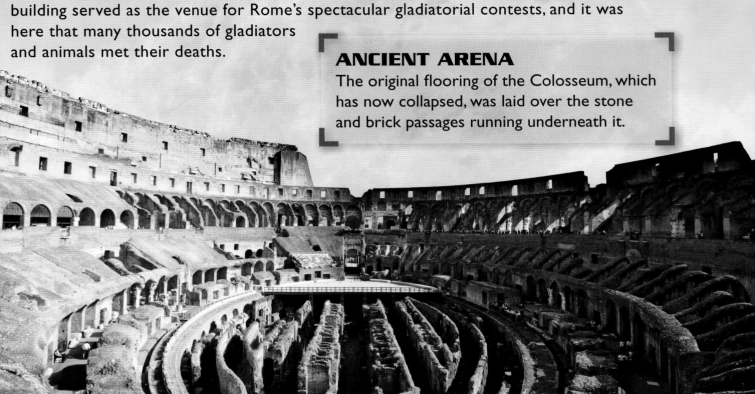

COMBAT STATS

The Colosseum

- **Date of construction:** begun 72 CE, finished 80 CE
- **Opening celebrations:** 100 days of gladiator fights
- **Maximum capacity:** 50,000 spectators
- **Wild animals slaughtered:** 9,000 in the 100-day opening celebrations alone
- **Most gladiators in one event:** 10,000 in 123 days of contests = 81 gladiators per day for half a year
- **Total number of people to die in the Colosseum:** 500,000 (estimated)

HORROR HUNTS

By the time of the first emperor, Augustus (ruled 27 BCE–14 CE), gladiatorial displays usually included mock animal hunts. Wild beasts were brought to Rome from Africa, Asia, and Europe. The animals were slaughtered as a gory warm-up before the main event.

BEASTS FOR SLAUGHTER

Exotic creatures were particularly popular with audiences. The animals killed in Roman arenas included bears, snakes, panthers, giraffes, crocodiles, and elephants.

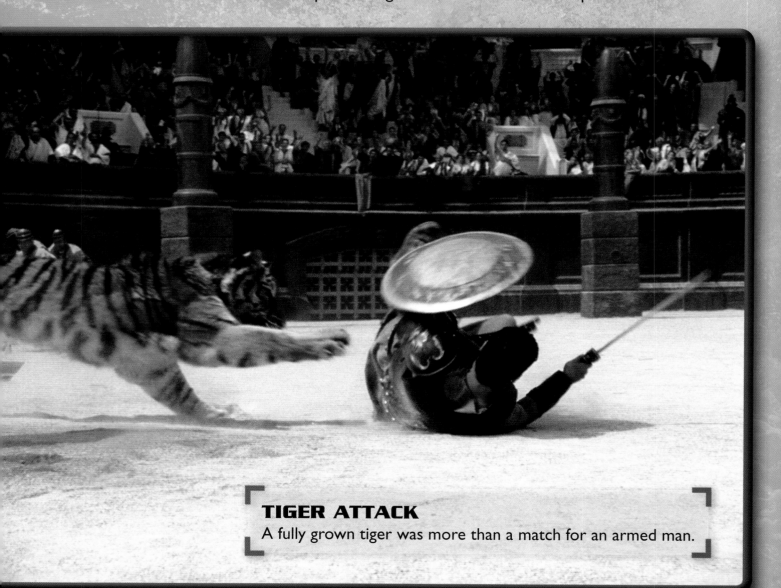

TIGER ATTACK
A fully grown tiger was more than a match for an armed man.

CONDEMNED TO THE BEASTS

Fully trained gladiators were rarely asked to fight animals. The usual beast-fighters (*bestiarii*) were untrained criminals or prisoners. From around 100 BCE, a common death penalty was *damnatio ad bestias*—condemned to the beasts. Instead of being hanged or crucified, the guilty person was thrown into an arena to be torn to pieces—usually by lions.

BEAST VS. GLADIATOR

A Roman mosaic from the fourth century CE depicts a gladiator fighting a wild beast.

COMBAT STATS

Order of play at a gladiatorial display

- **Six weeks in advance:** publicity leaflets and posters
- **Nightfall (7 p.m.) on day before the contest:** feast for gladiators
- **Sunrise (5 a.m.) on day of contest:** detailed programs (*libelli*) available
- **Early morning (9-10 a.m.):** procession into arena
- **Mid morning (11 a.m.):** wild beast hunt
- **Late morning (12 noon):** executions
- **Early afternoon (2 p.m.):** comedy shows, including mock fights
- **Afternoon (3-6 p.m.):** gladiatorial fights
- **Evening (7 p.m. onward):** female gladiatorial contests
- **Night (around 9 p.m.):** closing ceremony, music, and cleaning up begins

GLADIATORS ON WATER

In 46 BCE, the brilliant Roman general Julius Caesar introduced a new kind of gladiatorial contest. This was the mock naval battle or *naumachia*. The show involved real ships, packed with gladiators fighting each other on a lake or in a specially flooded arena.

BATTLESHIP

Roman warships were powered by sails, and in battle, rows of oars. A **trireme** had about 170 rowers and 60 soldiers on board. The aim was to **ram** an enemy vessel and sink it.

NAUMACHIA

In 42 BCE, Emperor Augustus built this special amphitheater on the right bank of the Tiber River for naval battles. It was approximately 580 x 390 yards (533 x 355 m) and had room for 30 warships with 3,000 fighting men on board.

COMBAT STATS

- **Largest recorded *naumachia*:** staged in 52 CE, by Emperor Claudius (ruled 41-54 CE), on Lake Fucino
- **Number of ships:** 24 full-size triremes (three banks of oars) and 26 **biremes** (two banks of oars)
- **Opposing fleets:** Rhodians (from Rhodes) vs. Sicilians, with 2 fleets of 25 ships each
- **Number on board:** 1,900 sailors and warriors, all criminals due to die, with each side commanded by one retired gladiator
- **Size of crowd:** 500,000
- **Battle salute:** before the battle, the competitors said to the emperor *"Morituri te salutant!"*—"Those who are about to die salute you!"

GREAT GLADIATORS

For some brave and skillful gladiators, success in the arena brought wealth, fame, and glory. For a few, it even brought freedom. Great gladiators were as famous in Rome as sports stars are today.

SPARTACUS

Spartacus, played here by Andy Whitfield in the television series *Spartacus: Blood and Sand* (2010), was one of the most famous gladiators of all. His story has inspired people ever since to fight against slavery, cruelty, and injustice.

FIGHTING TALK

The greatest gladiator

The Greek soldier Spartacus was sent to a gladiator school. In 73 BCE, he broke out and formed a rebel army of slaves and gladiators to fight against the Romans. Camped on Italy's Mount Vesuvius, they defeated several Roman forces sent against them. Eventually, in 71 BCE, they were defeated in the Battle of Sele. Spartacus' body was never found, and 6,000 of his followers were crucified.

REWARDS FOR SUCCESS

As well as prize money, a victorious gladiator would be given a crown or palm branch. If he had impressed the spectators with his skill and courage, they would sometimes throw down money for him. After a famous fight that ended in a draw in 80 CE, Emperor Titus gave both the gladiators—Priscus and Verus—their freedom.

HITS WITH THE GIRLS

Roman writers tell us that muscular gladiators were very popular with the women in the audience. The better-looking gladiators were never short of a date, although they had to keep the meetings secret.

CELEBRITY STATUS

Victorious gladiators often had huge numbers of fans, just like the actor Russell Crowe, seen here in the movie *Gladiator* (2000).

RISE AND FALL

At the height of their popularity in the first century CE, gladiatorial shows were costing around 180,000 *denarii* to put on—that's at least $400,000 in today's money. By the fourth century CE, the Roman Empire was poorer. Attitudes were changing, too, and the games gradually died out.

GLADIATOR COMMODUS

Emperor Commodus (ruled 161–192 CE), played here by Joaquin Phoenix in the film *Gladiator* (2000), was famous for entering the arena himself dressed as a gladiator. He butchered numerous animals, including elephants and giraffes.

SPIRALING COSTS

The first gladiatorial contests were organized by wealthy individuals. As the displays became more lavish, costs rose and they were largely taken over by the emperors. The shows became part of the government's entertainment program of public games or *ludi*. They were popular with many Roman emperors, who saw them as a way of winning approval and displaying their wealth and power.

CHRISTIANS IN THE ARENA

By around 100 CE, the Christian religion was spreading across the Roman Empire. Christians, who said gladiatorial fights were murder, were thrown to the lions for refusing to worship the emperor.

AN END TO CRUELTY

Many emperors, starting with Constantine in 325 CE, ordered gladiatorial shows to stop. Their commands were not always obeyed. In 365 CE, Christians were still being thrown to the lions for having an illegal faith. However, after Emperor Theodosius made Christianity the official religion of the empire, gladiatorial games gradually came to a stop.

CONDEMNED TO THE LIONS

A painting by Jean-Leon Gérôme (1883) depicts a group of Christian prisoners who have been condemned to face the lions.

FIGHTING TALK

Emperors in the arena

At least eight Roman emperors—Caligula, Caracalla, Commodus, Didius Julianus, Geta, Hadrian, Lucius Verus, and Titus—are said to have fought as gladiators. In fact, they all fought "staged" fights and never put themselves in real danger. Commodus, who called himself a *secutor*, shot 100 lions from a safe platform and cut the heads off ostriches.

GLOSSARY

amphitheater (meaning "place for all-round viewing") a circular or oval stadium with an arena in the center

arena a sand-covered circular or oval space at the center of an amphitheater where gladiators fought

barbarian the Roman word for non-Romans (literally "bearded ones")

bireme a warship with a sail and two banks of oars on each side

cavalry warriors who fought on horseback.

denarius a Roman coin (plural denarii)

emperor the head of an empire

empire a country or state and all the lands it controls

equites the Latin word for cavalry and for gladiators who fought on horseback

greave leg armor

Latin the language of the Romans

murmillo a gladiator with a fish-style crest on his helmet

professional working or fighting as one's job, for pay or other rewards

ram to use a large metal spike to smash an enemy ship

retiarius a gladiator who fought with a net and trident

samnite someone from Samnium in central Italy; also an early type of gladiator

secutor a type of gladiator that was trained to fight a retiarius

stirrup one of two metal hoops for a horse rider's feet, helping them balance

Thracian someone from the region of Thrace; also a type of gladiator

tribe a large group of people living together, like a clan

trident a lance with three prongs at the end

trireme a warship with a sail and three banks of oars on each side

FURTHER INFORMATION

Books

Ancient Rome by Simon James (Dorling Kindersley, 2008)

Gladiators and Roman Soldiers by Charlotte Guillain (Raintree, 2011)

Life as a Gladiator by Michael Burgan (Capstone Press, 2010)

The Roman Colosseum: The Story of the World's Most Famous Stadium and Its Deadly Games by Elizabeth Mann (Mikaya Press, 2006)

Web Sites

Beware—there are many unreliable sites on gladiators.

Gladiators

www.archive.archaeology.org/gladiators/

Archaeological Institute of America site with photos of original statues of gladiators from Ancient Rome. With features including "The Gladiator Diet" and "The Language of the Arena," a glossary section that explains Roman terms on gladiators, games, and gear such as weapons.

Roman Gladiators

www.historyforkids.org/learn/romans/games/circus.htm

Find out surprising facts about gladiators and gladiatorial games, chariot races, amphiteaters, and more. With links to photos, maps, and features.

Smithsonian: Secrets of the Colosseum

www.smithsonianmag.com/history-archaeology/Secrets-of-the-Colosseum.html

Read all about Rome's famous Colosseum, scene of the deadly gladiatorial contests. With amazing photographs and a 360-degree view feature.

Index